Original title:
The Ocean's Melody

Copyright © 2025 Creative Arts Management OÜ
All rights reserved.

Author: Juliana Wentworth
ISBN HARDBACK: 978-1-80587-282-5
ISBN PAPERBACK: 978-1-80587-752-3

## The Call of the Seabreeze

Seagulls squawk with endless glee,
As salty winds dance free.
Crabs do the cha-cha on the sand,
While fish flick tails, a finned band.

Splashing waves sing their tune,
Bubbles pop like a cartoon.
With every splash, a chuckle's made,
As the sun makes a sandcastle parade.

## **Triads of the Tide**

At low tide, clams wear tiny hats,
Barnacles groove like merry brats.
Waves declare a rhythmic beat,
While seaweed sways to a funky seat.

Starfish counting like they're in school,
Crabs share secrets, acting all cool.
The sea shimmies, a party so bright,
Mermaids brought chips, they serve all night.

## Fishing for Sounds

Fishermen toss lines to the sea,
But fish just giggle and flee.
A dolphin jumps, a splash and a grin,
Saying, "Why fish when you can swim?"

Octopuses play cards with delight,
While clownfish joke about their plight.
The sea's a carnival, not for naught,
Where laughter bubbles, and fun is caught.

## The Calm After the Storm

After a storm, the sea plays calm,
While sea turtles hum a soothing psalm.
Surfers arrive, riding the glass,
While jellyfish float, twirling with class.

Hermit crabs march in a parade,
Wearing shells that they've displayed.
Waves whisper softly, no need to worry,
As fish dart about in a playful flurry.

## Ballad of the Rolling Surf

The waves were dancing with delight,
As seagulls squawked, oh what a sight!
A fish wore shades, looking so cool,
While crabs held a race, breaking the rule.

With every splash, a giggle rang,
Shells wore hats, and the seaweed sang.
Mermaids tossed confetti from their hair,
Even the starfish joined in the fair!

## **Rhythms of the Raging Sea**

The tide came in with a boisterous laugh,
Chasing my towel, oh what a gaffe!
A dolphin jumped and high-fived a seal,
While jellyfish jived, giving a squeal.

The sun wore sunscreen, oh what a sight,
As surfers crashed in a comedic flight.
The water's a stage, ain't it a treat?
For fishy comedians with two left feet!

## Sonnet of the Swell

In the swell where the silliness brews,
Sea cucumbers form a quirky crew.
With waves that giggle and bubbles that wink,
A crab plays the banjo while mermaids drink.

The tides are plotting their playful schemes,
While tarpons dance to the rhythm of dreams.
Every splash says, "Hey, come have some fun!"
In this world of wonder, we've barely begun!

## **Wavesong in the Moonlight**

Under the moon, the sea sings loud,
With fish that floss and a crab so proud.
Octopuses juggling shells with style,
While turtles play tag, going mile by mile.

Dancing in currents, the sea stars twinkle,
A clam tells a joke, and the waves all crinkle.
As laughter ripples through creature and foam,
The night by the water feels just like home!

## **Underwater Whispers**

Bubbles talk in secret tones,
With fishy giggles and silly groans.
Seashells gossip, they make a fuss,
While sea cucumbers ride the bus.

Starfish spin a dance, quite a sight,
While crabs wear hats, oh what a fright!
Octopuses juggle, not a care,
In this bubbly world, laughter's in air.

## Tidepool Tunes

Barnacles sing in clunky rhymes,
As seagulls laugh, they steal the times.
Clams tap their shells in rhythmic grace,
While wiggly worms join the race.

Jellyfish bounce like jelly on toast,
With sea urchins joining, they're quite a host.
The seaweed sways, a funky dance,
In the tidepool here, you'll take a chance.

## Sails and Seafoam

A pirate ship with a wobbly mast,
Chased by dolphins, oh what a blast!
With salty sea shanties, they sing along,
While mermaids giggle, so full of song.

The sails flap wildly, caught in the breeze,
While fish do pirouettes, aiming to please.
With every splash and foam that flies,
Laughter echoes beneath bright skies.

## A Canvas of Blue

In a world painted with hues so bright,
Seagulls play tag, oh what a sight!
Whales pull pranks, with splashes of cheer,
Creating waves of laughter here.

Coral reefs host a hilarious ball,
As clowns in costume, they're having a ball!
In this canvas of blue, with joy on display,
The sea's funny side always makes my day.

## **Tides' Heartbeat**

The tide came in with a cheeky grin,
A crab danced off like he's in a spin.
Seagulls squawked in a silly choir,
While fish played tag in their underwater fire.

A starfish wore a bright pink hat,
Said, 'Behold my fabulous aquatic spat!'
The waves all chuckled, a bubbly affair,
And seaweed swayed as if to declare.

## A Nautical Nocturne

The moon beamed down on a fishy scene,
Where dolphins practiced their breakdance routine.
An octopus juggled seashells with flair,
While a clam sang loudly, without any care.

The plankton twinkled like stars out of reach,
As a whale tried to rhyme in a lyrical speech.
The night was alive with giggles and splashes,
Even the barnacles joined in with their clashes.

## **Reef Harmonies**

In the reef, a band had begun to play,
With trumpet fish leading the jolly parade.
Corals swayed to the rhythm of glee,
While anemones danced, just wait and see!

A sea turtle waltzed, round and round,
To a tune made of bubbles that floated sound.
The snails brought a beat, slow but groovy,
As everyone jived to their underwater movie.

## Chasing the Currents

With a splash and a dash, the current took flight,
Sardines swam fast, trying to ignite.
A wise old fish shrugged, said, 'What a race!'
While the sea urchins chuckled, enjoying their space.

A turtle was lost, said, 'Which way to the fun?'
As fish swirled around like they were on a run.
The current just giggled and swirled with delight,
As they all sped off into the moonlit night.

## The Song of Sirens

In waves they sing, a quirky tune,
Fish dance in line, beneath the moon.
Seagulls giggle, in the breeze,
Sandy toes and salty cheese.

Their laughter bounces off the shore,
Crabs in tuxedos, crave for more.
Shells are clapping, a vibrant band,
Jellyfish jiving, on the sand.

With every splash, a splash of glee,
Seashells joke, 'Come dance with me!'
Even the seaweed joins the fray,
In this daft and splashy play.

And when the tide starts to hide,
Fish drag their tails, on a joyride.
Mermaids chuckle, flip their hair,
While dolphins leap, without a care.

**Undercurrents of Love**

A fish fell hard, for a crab so sweet,
He brought her pearls, a tasty treat.
She said, 'You're cute, but crabby too,'
He winked, 'Well, love's not easy, boo!'

They met at dawn, under the sea,
He tripped on sand, oh what a spree!
She rolled her eyes, but couldn't resist,
With every laugh, they sealed their tryst.

In seaweed fields, they twirled so bright,
Starfish watched on, a comical sight.
Octopus grinned, holding his drinks,
'Love's not all pearls, it's also winks.'

Through currents swift, they danced along,
Crabby giggles in a silly song.
Nothing's fishy, just love's embrace,
In this wavy, warm, funny space.

## The Call of Distant Horizons

A gull took flight, with dreams so grand,
Planning trips to far-off land.
Challenging waves to keep him still,
He squawked, 'Ahoy! I've got time to kill!'

He landed quick, on an old seal's back,
'Tell me tales of the pirate's attack!'
The seal just snorted, 'What a flop,
I'll tell you tales, but don't make me stop!'

With treasures found in pockets of sea,
They laughed aloud, just wild and free.
'Let's race the tides!' the gull did cheer,
Waves rolled in, full of friendly jeer.

Their voices rose, a jovial sound,
As jellybeans flopped, all around.
Adventure calls with such absurd glee,
Horizons wide, for you and me!

## Resounding Ripples

A pebble plunked, a curious start,
Waves rippled out, art from the heart.
Fishes giggled, made a new game,
Bubbles danced, in water's name.

They played charades with a bright starfish,
Who claimed to grant one crazy wish.
But when a fish asked for more scales,
Starfish chuckled, 'Let's swap our tails!'

A seahorse snorted, 'What's the deal?
These crazy antics just feel surreal!'
Yet laughter echoed out for miles,
Coral reefs junking their serious styles.

With every splash, the silliness grew,
Crustaceans conga, yes, that's true!
In playful waves, they found delight,
Ripples of happiness, all through the night.

## Moonlit Muses

Under the moon, the fish do dance,
Jellyfish twirl in a slimy prance.
A crab in a tux, oh what a sight,
Claps his claws with all his might.

Seagulls gossip, they squawk and squall,
Trying to steal the clownfish's ball.
Starfish tell jokes, but they're just so flat,
Even the octopus thinks they're a brat.

As waves crash loud with a bubbly cheer,
Shells giggle softly, they've had a beer.
Turtles on surfboards, oh what a thrill,
Sliding on waves, they've got the skill!

So let us laugh at the silly sea show,
Where barnacles beatbox, and mermaids flow.
Here under the moon, with sparkle and glee,
Life in the sea is pure comedy.

## **Coral Requiem**

Coral reefs sing, but with a croak,
Fish in tuxedos play card games and joke.
A shrimp pulls pranks on a passing shark,
While snails debate if it's light or dark.

Clownfish juggle, they're the circus stars,
Bubbles fly up, they'll reach for Mars.
Anemones chuckle at the jelly's plight,
As they drift through currents, lost in the night.

The seaweed sways, in a funny dance,
Seahorses twirl as if in a trance.
A pufferfish bursts, what a sight to see,
Turns out he's just shy! Who would agree?

So let's raise our shells for this quirky crew,
To the laughs and the gags that we all knew.
In the underwater realm, where laughter is grand,
Each wave brings a smile, isn't life just planned?

## **Driftwood Dreams**

Driftwood whispers secrets of the sea,
While crabs build castles, just a bit free.
A dolphin dons shades for a sunbathe glow,
Flips and splashes in a hilarious show.

Walruses waddle, with blubbered pride,
Sharing tall tales of their ocean ride.
While otters hold hands, in a charming way,
Fighting to keep the seaweed at bay.

A turtle's slow, but with some flair,
He'll beat you at racing if you dare!
With sea cucumbers rolling, all jiggly and sweet,
They beat the sea urchins with their groovy beat.

They dream of adventures, under waves so bright,
Chasing fast currents, into the night.
For every driftwood dream brings a play,
In the depths of the sea where fun's here to stay.

## Oceanic Chords

Seashells play music, a funny tune,
Mermaids sing softly, under the moon.
With dolphins as backup, they leap out bright,
Creating a concert, a truly grand night.

Starfish on stage, strum with a wink,
Octopus drummers tap out the beat, pink.
Catchy melodies rise with the tide,
Even crabs in the crowd can't help but glide.

Seagulls are hecklers, though they do try,
To crack the best jokes, they give it a high.
"Your seaweed is green, and your scales are blue!"
Echoes ring 'round, what a cheeky crew!

As the final note splashes, a wave of applause,
The fish throw their fins, causing joyful jaws.
In the concert of life, every chord finds a way,
In this symphony's laughter, we all want to stay.

## Song of the Surf

Waves crash down with a splish-splash,
Seagulls giggle in a mad dash,
There's a fish wearing sunglasses bright,
Thinking it's a party, what a sight!

The crab on the shore does a little dance,
Trying to impress a passing whale's glance,
The tide rolls in with a frothy grin,
While clams dream of where they've been.

A dolphin juggles shells with flair,
As seaweed whispers, 'Ain't life fair?'
Starfish play cards on the ocean floor,
While octopuses serve fish galore!

Oh, the tide is a playful friend indeed,
With sandy toes and a sparkle of freed,
Sailing along with a skip and a laugh,
In waters where we all find our path!

## **Nautical Nocturne**

Underneath the moon's shiny beam,
Mermaids conspire in a fishy dream,
With bubbles that pop and tickle their toes,
They sing to the stars, in silly prose.

The lobster plays tunes on a rusty shell,
While jellyfish dance, oh can't you tell?
Crabs wear hats made of seaweed strands,
Tossing sea cucumbers in festive bands.

A dolphin snores in a hammock of kelp,
While sea turtles grin and yelp your help,
The plankton glow in a giggly fit,
As plankton plans a glow-in-the-dark skit!

With laughter that echoes through the deep,
They invite you to join their fun and leap,
In this underwater carnival so bright,
With costumes, confetti, and pure delight!

## Secrets of the Seaweed

Hidden treasures in the sea's green fray,
Seaweed whispers, 'Come laugh and play!'
With secrets tangled in every strand,
Join the sea creatures, it's all so grand!

A crab spills tea with a clam so shy,
While joking seagulls swoop from the sky,
The sea cucumbers gossip in rows,
As they discuss what nobody knows!

Anemones wiggle in colorful hues,
Swaying and dancing in ocean blues,
The stars keep a lookout with a wink,
While fish trade rumors over a drink.

Oh, tangled tales in the marine light,
Bring smiles and giggles, not a fright,
So dive down deep and take a peek,
At the secrets the seaweed loves to speak!

## Bubbles of Bliss

Bubbles rise with a playful pop,
Tickling the octopus as he hops,
Fish swap jokes in a watery race,
While a unicorn fish hides its face.

The sea anemone waves hello,
As the tide sways to and fro,
Surfers giggle on their bright boards,
While dolphins practice their silly chords.

A whale sings songs that make fish dance,
And every crab dreams of a romance,
With bubbles of bliss floating around,
Making smiles on the ocean ground.

So come join the fun in the splashy spray,
Where laughter echoes and fish play,
In a world where joy is never far,
Just follow the giggles beneath the star!

## **Ballad of the Waves**

The waves dance like they've got a tune,
They splash around, making quite a rune.
A crab on the shore tries to bust a move,
But slips in the foam—what a silly groove!

Seagulls squawk, joining the beat,
They dive and they swoop, oh what a feat.
A fish pokes its head, wondering why,
As laughter bubbles up to the sky.

A dolphin jumps, flips with a grin,
Says, "Join in the fun! Let the games begin!"
But a seal rolls over, all belly and blubber,
Its attempt at a flip? Oh, what a blunder!

So come join the fun where the waves are bright,
With creatures so silly that take to flight.
Dance with the tide, make a splash and play,
In this watery world, we laugh the day away!

## Serenade of the Sea

The sea plays a song of splashes and grins,
As shells gossip softly, about sea urchin sins.
A lobster hops like it's in a ballet,
While a clam clamors, 'Please, not today!'

With each little swell, there's a jig and a jiggle,
An octopus sways, with a dance and a wiggle.
Turtles in flippers, looking quite chic,
Stroll down the beach like they own the peak.

Fish are comedians, all trying to wow,
One tells a joke and it's a big wow-wow!
A starfish chuckles, while stuck on a rock,
"Flip me over, I'm missing the clock!"

The seaweed joins in, with a giddy old sway,
As all sea creatures join in the play.
Every splash tells a tale from the sea,
In this funny world, just you wait and see!

## Echoes Beneath the Surface

Beneath the waves, there's a ruckus at school,
Where fish play tag, thinking it's cool.
A moray eel sneezes, what a loud honk!
And bubbles go up, like a silly prank, honk honk!

Anemones wave, with arms all a-flail,
While a flatfish lies low, trying to fail.
"Don't see me now!" it mutters and grins,
But a curious crab whispers, "Sorry, my fins!"

A pufferfish jokes, swells up with pride,
"Bet you can't catch me!" it chuckles, then hides.
But a passing whale rolls its eye with a laugh,
"Can't form a joke with a pointy old staff!"

So listen closely to the giggles below,
The sea's a party with a comedic flow.
In every ripple, laughter finds its place,
Echoes of joy in this watery space.

## Chasing the Horizon

The horizon giggles, running away,
While sailors on boats try hard to say:
"Catch us a glimpse, oh line of the blue!"
But it ducks and it dives, always out of view.

The mermaids are laughing, flipping their hair,
Holding a contest—who can float in mid-air?
A fish joins the chase, all fins and scales,
Trying to figure out funny old tales.

As sunsets spread colors, they paint with a brush,
The ocean erupts with a humorous hush.
A dolphin shouts out, "Hey, let's race!"
But trips on a wave, what a slippery place!

So if you're out there, and a wave gives a cheer,
Know that the journey is filled with good cheer.
Chasing horizons, we dance in the sun,
With laughter and joy, in this splashing fun!

## **Melodies from the Mariner's Dream**

A fish in a tux, doing a jig,
The seaweed sways, it's quite the gig.
Octopus bands play all night long,
With crabs in the crowd, singing along.

Dolphins tap dance, flipping with flair,
While seagulls complain, it's just not fair.
A pirate's off-key, with a grog in hand,
His parrot just squawks to join the band.

Starfish in shades, lounging about,
Think they're too cool, but they just pout.
Each wave is a note, each splash a beat,
As laughter bubbles, it's quite the feat.

So when you're by shore, let loose and play,
Join in the fun, it's a sea-side ballet.
With fishy free-styling and jolly old whales,
The humor and joy ride the salty gales.

## Symphony of Shell and Sand

Seashells forming a quirky band,
Each playing notes from grains of sand.
A crab with a kazoo, what a sight!
Piper fish blow, tunes out of fright.

Seagulls squawk off-key, it's a blast,
While turtles keep tempo, slow and fast.
A conch serves as the conductor's hat,
Leading the sea in a wiggly chat.

Waves crash in laughter, a bubbly sound,
As plankton twirl and dance all around.
Each tide brings giggles, a watery cheer,
While sea cucumbers join in the sphere.

A laughter-filled concert beneath the sun,
Where jellyfish jiggle just for fun.
So if you feel blue, just scratch the sand,
And hear the joy from this merry band.

## Enchanted Waters

In the deep, where silliness swims,
Mermaids giggle in sparkly whims.
With a splash there's a joke, a punchline too,
As mermen juggle, and bubbles pursue.

Nemo tells tales of a fishy plight,
Caught in a net but danced outta sight.
A whale gives a wink, "I'll take the lead,"
"I'll sing a deep song, so follow my creed!"

Crabs throw a party with clam-shell snacks,
While dolphins surf waves like crazy hacks.
The night brings a glow, a phosphorescent spree,
As laughter erupts from beneath the sea.

So if you're feeling down on dry land,
Just remember the joy from the fishy strand.
The depths hold great wonders, both funny and bright,
In those enchanted waters, everything's light.

## Echoing Under the Sea

A sea turtle's yawn echoes far and wide,
As fish swim by, with eyebrows held high.
"Did you hear that?" they giggle and glee,
"Under the waves, we're as light as the sea!"

Jellyfish glow like disco lights,
While clowns of the sea put on silly sights.
With a flip and a flop, they make quite the scene,
As laughter dances, all crisp and serene.

Anemones sway, throwing shade with flair,
While seahorses gossip, but we don't care.
The shrimp form a conga, they've just got the knack,
Groovin' with shells, they never hold back.

So if life feels heavy, take a dive,
To where the giggles and gurgles thrive.
Down deep, there's a rhythm, a jolly decree,
Echoing laughter, forever carefree.

## Journey through the Blue

A fish wore a hat, oh what a sight,
He danced in the waves, full of delight.
With bubbles for laughter, and fins to groove,
He swam in a circle, trying to prove.

A crab played the drums on a tin can tight,
While octopuses juggled from morning to night.
Seahorses twirled, in a comical race,
Each flip and each splash, a wet slapstick chase.

The whale tried to sing, but sounded a croak,
The dolphins all giggled, shared a good joke.
They splashed through the sun, like a joyful parade,
In the blue belly laugh, they all serenade.

## Rhapsody of the Reef

A lobster in shades sipped tea on the shore,
While a clownfish juggled with shells by the score.
Starfish made wishes with a flip and a spin,
Each secret they shared made the bubbles begin.

A turtle named Timmy forgot how to swim,
He rolled on the rocks, thought it was a whim.
A pufffish was giggling, full of good cheer,
Blowing up bubbles that popped out of sheer.

A ray caught a joke on a slick, wavy ride,
While seagulls quarreled, not wanting to hide.
The reef echoed laughter, a chorus so bright,
In the playful embrace of each shimmering light.

## Beacons in the Mist

A lighthouse cat napped, on the top of his perch,
While seagulls below planned a hilarious search.
They launched little pranks on the boats passing by,
And laughed at the sailors who jumped with a cry.

A pelican clown had a big fish to gulp,
He struggled to swallow, made quite the clump.
Nearby, a walrus wore glasses, so thick,
He waddled for miles, to perform a new trick.

The foghorn sang tunes, with a whimsical twist,
Each note made them giggle, the waves never missed.
As laughter alarmed, they brightened the gloom,
In the harbor's sweet heart, where the chuckles bloom.

## **Tidal Harmonies**

The tides danced and cavorted, a whimsical waltz,
With crabs doing twist moves, despite all their faults.
An eel slipped and slid on a banana peel,
As fish in tuxedos took turns to squeal.

A jellyfish floated with flair and with style,
While clownfish cracked jokes that made all of them smile.
The waves held their breath, for a splash had to come,
As laughter erupted, like bubbles, it spun.

A dolphin named Chuck, with a sense of finesse,
Played a tune on a shell, a sweet kind of mess.
With frolic and fun, they swam through the night,
In the tides' merry dance, full of joy and delight.

## Whispers of the Tide

The waves they dance, oh what a treat,
A fish in a hat says, "Can't be beat!"
Seagulls squawk with a comic flair,
As crabs in tuxedos boast and stare.

A starfish winks, quite full of cheer,
While dolphins giggle as they steer.
Sandcastles crumble in fits of glee,
"Oops! That was not meant for me!"

Shells gossip softly about the tide,
A hermit crab claims, "I've got style!"
The seaweed sways with a cheeky grin,
As clownfish prance with a silly spin.

So come on down and join the fun,
Where laughter bubbles like the sun.
The shore's alive with chatter and song,
In this big blue realm, we all belong.

## Chords of the Deep

In the deepest blue, a band does play,
A shrimp on drums says, "Let's groove today!"
A whale with a saxophone, oh what a sight,
Blows bubbles of music, pure delight.

The octopus strums on a seaweed guitar,
While jellyfish glow like a disco star.
The sea cucumbers shuffle and sway,
"Footloose in the reef!" they proudly say.

Surfers ride on waves like a tune,
Singin' to dolphins beneath the moon.
"Catch this rhythm," the seafoam giggles,
As currents dance and the starfish wiggles.

With every splash, a note takes flight,
The ocean rocks out, what a silly sight!
From the tide pools to the deep blue sea,
Join the band, come and be free!

## Symphony Beneath Waves

In the currents' sway, the fish do jam,
With flutes made of shells and a seaweed slam.
A playful turtle conducts the show,
While seahorses twirl, oh what a flow!

Coral reefs hum with tones so bright,
A bass fish cracks jokes that are out of sight.
The barnacles tap on a clam's old drum,
While kelp dancers twist, they won't feel glum.

A pufferfish blows up for the big finale,
Vibrating tunes through the underwater rally.
The sea anemones wave with finesse,
As fish chorus "We love this mess!"

So let the symphony fill every shore,
With laughter and joy, who could ask for more?
In this aquatic hall, laughter's the key,
Join the underwater jubilee!

## Lullabies of the Seafloor

Beneath the waves, where the sea snails hum,
A clam sings softly, oh how it strums!
Starfish twirl in their cozy beds,
While ghost crabs tell tales, spinning their threads.

The sea urchins share secrets at dusk,
"Did you hear about that fish? Quite a husk!"
Tangled in kelp, a sea turtle snores,
While waves softly lap against ancient shores.

Anemones sway, calming the night,
With lullabies sung beneath soft moonlight.
A whale whispers, "Dream big and far,"
As sea otters float by, sipping from jars.

With each lilting note from the deep,
All creatures hum lullabies as they sleep.
In this underwater realm, peace takes its hold,
Where tales of the sea are lovingly told.

## **Liquid Dreams**

Fish in tuxedos swim with flair,
Jellybeans bouncing everywhere.
Crabs tap dance on sandy floors,
While seagulls squawk as they explore.

A dolphin juggles shells with ease,
While plankton giggle in the breeze.
Octopus rock bands play a tune,
Underneath a bright, cartoon moon.

## Dance of the Gentle Waves

Waves do the cha-cha, oh what a sight,
Seashells shimmy left and right.
A starfish twirls in eight steps wide,
While crabs cheer on from the tide.

The sunbeams clap on water's skin,
Splashing rhythms where dreams begin.
Seaweed sways like a funky hat,
Who knew that fish were cool like that?

## **Chants of the Coast**

The sand sings songs of giggles and glee,
With sandcastles smiling back at me.
Seagulls crack jokes, perched on their thrones,
And flip-flops dance with silly tones.

Mermaids gossip with a splash and flip,
While walruses tease with a comedic quip.
Shells whisper secrets, oh how they tease,
As the tides read stories in the breeze.

## Tempest's Serenade

A storm cloud rumbles with a funny tune,
As lightning dances like a silly goon.
Raindrops giggle as they tumble down,
Making puddles that wear a frown.

Waves crash and bash with a playful cheer,
While sea monsters laugh, showing no fear.
Wind joins the fun, howling a jest,
Nature's commotion puts humor to the test.

## Waves of Future Tides

The seagulls squawk with flair,
Shouting jokes from salty air.
Fish flip-flop; they seem to grin,
Dancing waves just can't keep in.

Sandcastles stand with pride,
Guarding treasures from the tide.
But a wave comes with a smile,
Knocking down work in a while.

Crabs wear shirts, pretend to strut,
Caught in laughter, they just mutt.
"Don't pinch me!" cries a clown fish,
As they splash for a silly wish.

With surfboards made of cheese,
Riders glide with goofy ease.
Every swell brings giggles loud,
In this joyful splashy crowd.

## Currents of Love

A dolphin flips with a wink,
Playing games under the pink.
Turtles glide without a care,
While jellyfish float in the air.

Starfish hold a dance-off scene,
With octopuses dressed in green.
They twirl and swirl in the bay,
Making every fish shout hooray!

Anemones tickle the toes,
Of passing fish in silly rows.
Their joyful dance is hard to snare,
Leaving smiles everywhere.

Underwater hearts with glee,
Make bubbles of pure jubilee.
Love is found in corals bright,
As sea creatures bid goodnight.

## Whispering Waters

Waves gossip in a silly tone,
As clams sit gossiping alone.
"Did you hear what happened today?"
A crab laughed as he scuttled away.

Mermaids giggle, sing and sway,
While octopuses shuffle and play.
"Can you believe that splash!" they cheer,
As a wave crashes, bringing cheer.

"Catch my bubbles!" a fish shouts,
As fun and laughter spins about.
"Hold my fin!" roars a seal,
Tumbling in, it's a goofing reel.

With every wake, a laugh is born,
From the sea, chaos is sworn.
Each ripple carries a joke,
In these waters, fun is bespoke.

## **Dockside Duet**

Fishermen sing with a quirky beat,
As they dance on the dock with feet.
"Reel it in!" one shouts with glee,
"Catch a fish that sings like me!"

Pelicans bob with a quirky grace,
Hoping for snacks in this fishy place.
"Why did the fish blush?" they tease,
"Because it saw the ocean's freeze!"

Ropes holding boats sway in time,
While seagulls croon their funny rhyme.
"Just wait 'til we catch a big one!"
"We're the best, and we haven't begun!"

With laughter weaving through the air,
Fishing tales beyond compare.
Dockside life, a rhythmic spree,
Where friendship and silliness roam free.

## Secrets of the Abyss

Fish in tuxedos, they dance with glee,
Jellyfish giggle, oh what a spree!
A crab with a hat tells tales with flair,
While sea turtles snicker, without a care.

Schools of sardines do a silly parade,
With clam shells clapping, they're unafraid.
A whale sings songs, but they're off-key,
As octopuses juggle, it's quite the spree!

## Swaying with the Current

Surfers in bubbles, riding the tide,
Seagulls with sunglasses, surfing with pride.
Crabs with their surfboards, gleefully shout,
As waves of laughter echo about.

Seashells collect secrets, snickers, and jokes,
While dolphins flip tricks, wearing bright cloaks.
A starfish takes selfies, striking a pose,
As fish throw confetti, everyone knows!

## **Melodies of Distant Shores**

Seashell trumpets blare with delight,
Clams tap dance, oh what a sight!
The wind joins in, with a giggling sound,
Making waves bounce high off the ground.

Upon the shore, the sandcastles cheer,
Mermaids joke as they swim near.
A crab recites poetry, oh so bold,
As waves whisper secrets, stories retold.

## The Sea's Sweet Symphony

Polka-dotted fish hold a disco ball,
While conchs are the DJs, spinning it all.
Gulls are the backup, flapping away,
As dolphins breakdance, stealing the day.

A clownfish winks, plays peek-a-boo,
As sardines pop popcorn, watching the crew.
The rhythm of bubbles, the laughter of tides,
In this salty circus, joy never hides.

**Symphony of Salt and Sand**

The seagull squawks, it starts to sing,
A crab in a dance, doing its thing.
With shells for drums and waves for tune,
We laugh as jellyfish float like balloons.

A beach ball bounces, oh what a sight,
A toddler's giggle from morning till night.
Flip-flops slap in a silly parade,
While sunscreen battles the beachside brigade.

The tide rolls in with a slap and a tickle,
Dancing with sand, oh what a fickle.
Shouting, "Watch out!" as waves rush and roam,
Stealing our towels like they're on loan.

Each splash brings joy, a chuckle or two,
The seagulls complain, they squawk out, "Boo!"
Laughter echoes, a jolly old band,
In this salty symphony upon the sand.

## Rhythms of the Rolling Tide

The waves clap hands, a splashy cheer,
As rubber ducks float in without fear.
A surfboard sneezes from salt and sun,
Waves giggle, "Come play, it's all in good fun!"

A sandcastle wobbles, ready to fall,
"It's a palace!" we shout, proud and tall.
With moats and flags made of shells and sticks,
The tide says, "Nice job! Now watch for my tricks!"

Seashells gossip in whispers so fleet,
As kids dig deep with sandy, small feet.
A mermaid giggles from under the foam,
"Join my ocean, come! It's never a chore!"

But watch out for waves that sneak in your shoes,
They'll steal your snacks and leave you with blues.
"Hey, give it back!" we laugh, and we glide,
Chasing the rhythms of the rolling tide.

## Nautical Lullaby

The stars in the sky wink down at the sea,
As crickets fill in with a soft harmony.
A ship made of coconuts sails in the night,
While fish tap their fins in soft, gentle light.

A giant octopus plays the guitar,
With bubble-blowers swirling, we cheer from afar.
"Play us a song," we laugh with delight,
As sea cucumbers dance, twinkling so bright.

Whales hum low, deep as a drum,
While a school of fish wiggles, "Don't be so glum!"
Going to bed on this floating cloud,
Dreaming of sea shanties, soft and loud.

The tide rocks us gently, lulled in the bass,
With jellyfish bobbing, oh, what a grace!
We drift off to sleep in our sandy La-Z-Bee,
The ocean's sweet lullaby calls out to me.

## Harmonies of the Blue

Under the waves, a concert unfolds,
With sea stars twinkling, like stories retold.
Clams snap their shells to a rhythmic beat,
While dolphins spin high in a dance so sweet.

A treasure chest bursts with shiny delight,
Gold coins that jingle, oh what a sight!
"Hey, who's stealing my pearls?" a clam does shout,
As hard-headed sea turtles swim round about.

The seaweed sways like a soft, green brush,
As turtles glide by in a gentle hush.
"Join in the fun!" cries a crab with a cheer,
As squishy sea anemones wriggle near.

With fishy harmonies, the ocean sings loud,
As we laugh along, feeling oh-so-proud.
In waves of laughter, let's dance and twirl,
In the watery world, where fun is a whirl.

## **Tidal Serenades**

Waves crash and splash, oh what a sight,
A dolphin does flips, pure delight!
Seagulls squawk, with a cheeky flair,
As crabs dance sideways without a care.

A fish in a tux, with a top hat neat,
Says, "Nice to meet you! Want to eat?"
A clam replays yesterday's news,
While the starfish giggles at its own shoes.

Chasing my hat that's stuck on a wave,
I laugh as I dive, feeling so brave!
The conch shell tells jokes, just for a laugh,
And you can't help but share in the gaff.

So come ride the rhythm, don't hesitate,
Life's like a splash, it's never too late!
Each tide brings laughter, a quirky sound,
In this seaside concert, joy can be found.

## Sails in a Sea of Sound

The boat rocks gently like it's asleep,
While the fish crack jokes, oh what a leap!
A parrot sings loudly, off-key as heck,
While I try hard not to fall off the deck.

With sails that flap like a big loud grin,
The wind joins in, playing its din.
A crab with a violin, so oddly refined,
Plays tunes that are wacky, but oh so well-timed.

Blue whales join in, singing bass so low,
While dolphins do flips, putting on a show.
The captain's hat flies, caught in the breeze,
As I chase it down, laughing with ease.

In this wavy party, each ripple is fun,
As we sail through verses, one by one!
Let's dance on the waves, bring smiles and cheer,
In this sea of sound, we'll stay without fear.

## Whispers of the Deep

Bubbles rise up, with gossip so grand,
A jellyfish winks, it's got a soft hand.
The octopus juggles, all eight arms in play,
As fish laugh and clap in their own little way.

A turtle named Louie swims like a pro,
Says, "I'm only slow because I like the flow!"
The shrimp form a band with shells that they bang,
While the seaweed sways, doing the tango twang.

Anemones giggle, they tickle and tease,
As crabs hold a meeting, determined to please.
A shark in a bow tie takes a sip of tea,
Says, "It's quite dapper, wouldn't you agree?"

The deep is alive with chuckles and fun,
Moments like this, they weigh a ton!
Join in this laughter, let friendship swim deep,
In the world below, let's joyfully leap.

**Tides in Tune**

Sunrise wakes up with a giggle so bright,
As waves roll in, all ready for flight.
Seashells are whispering tales of the day,
While flounders in bowties dance in a fray.

With surfboards on waves, the seals come to play,
Riding high rollers, oh what a display!
A lobster in shades thinks he's quite the guy,
And a crab with a polka dot tie gleefully sigh.

Mermaids tell puns that are bubbly and fun,
As the sun dips low, it's not yet done.
The tide brings on giggles, a funny parade,
While sardines line up for the greatest charade.

So join in the chorus, let laughter be found,
In this world of whimsy, we twirl around!
Each wave brings joy, a jubilant boon,
As we dance to the rhythm, under the moon.

## **Dreams on the Ocean's Edge**

Seagulls squawk like clowns in the sky,
Wave-washed toes, oh my, oh my!
A crab in a tux, dancing with flair,
He thinks he's a star, do we really care?

Fishy perfume wafts through the breeze,
Sandy sandwiches, oh, what a tease!
Children giggle, they're not so discreet,
Splashing their parents, oh, isn't that sweet?

Beach balls zoom, like rockets in flight,
A seagull steals fries, what a greedy sight!
Flip-flops flapping on the hot, sunny ground,
Sunscreen's a mess, it's all over town.

As twilight approaches, the jokes start anew,
A sandcastle fest, with moats made of goo.
With laughter that echoes and seashells that sing,
Who knew that the shore could be such a fling?

## Lullabies of Salted Air

Waves giggle softly, a tickle of foam,
As crabs hold a concert far away from home.
A dolphin's flip flops, they sparkle and shine,
Making fishy friends, all in good time.

Starfish plotting, they gather in crowds,
Making pacts under silvery clouds.
"Let's start a band," one clam starts to shout,
"Just need some more shells and a little more clout!"

Jellyfish waltz, all dressed up for a ball,
Ballooning in rhythm, they float in the hall.
Tide pools are lakes for a frog concert,
With laughter and bubbles, it's quite an exert!

So sing to the sunset, with the breeze in your hair,
Let humor be washed with the salt in the air.
Dance like the waves, let your worries take flight,
For the sea's lullabies fill the heart every night.

## **Crashing Crescendos**

A wave rolls in with a thunderous cheer,
It knocks down the sandcastle—a classic frontier!
Laughter erupts as the towers collapse,
Tiny hands wave, "Let's build some mishaps!"

Seashells gossip, all nestled in sand,
About a lone fish who dreamed of a band.
Guitar made of coral, drumbeats of foam,
As they play on the beach, they just can't go home!

The starfish gets crazy, tries an oompah-pah,
While the octopus conducts from beneath a straw.
Each note a splash, every laugh a delight,
As the sun waves goodbye, they jam through the night.

So let down your hair, wiggle your toes,
Join the laughter where the tide really flows.
For the crashing crescendos make spirits feel bold,
This seaside symphony is a sight to behold!

## Horizons of Harmony

Waves crash in rhythm, like musical notes,
Seagulls swoop down, they must be the coats.
With surfboards like chariots, they race through the sea,
Chasing the dreams that float wild and free.

The sun sets in colors of giggles and glee,
While a crab in a bowtie sings karaoke!
Fish flash their fins, dancing under the tide,
With laughter that bubbles, they dance side by side.

Now sand angels whisper sweet secrets of fun,
As flip-flops collide in the rush of the sun.
With friends all around, let's do a parade,
As the waves rise like music, together we wade.

So embrace the silliness, let it unfold,
With horizons of harmony where stories are told.
From giggles to splashes, let joy be your song,
For in this ocean charm, we all truly belong!

## **Harmonics in Blue**

The fish wear hats, it's true,
Dancing to a funky tune.
Jellyfish with jelly shoes,
Making waves, oh what a swoon!

Seagulls strut on sandy toes,
Pretending to be all the pros.
We built castles, wind just blows,
Sandy moats, but where's our hose?

Crabs play cards beneath the sun,
Their poker face, it's pretty fun.
They rarely lose, they're on the run,
I'll beat them next, just need a bun!

Turtles playing hide and seek,
Sneaky shells, they play for keeps.
Underwater giggles peak,
As each fish takes their funny leaps!

## Serenade of Salt and Sun

A clam sings out a silly tune,
While doodlebugs dance with a spoon.
The sun throws rays, a golden boon,
Baked tan fins of a rubber tune!

Octopuses throw a fancy ball,
With eight guests who say, 'Let's have a haul!'
They twist and whirl, oh what a sprawl,
Around the coral castle hall!

Waves crash in with splashes bright,
Each one a giggle, pure delight.
Sand castles wobble, hold on tight,
Or they'll wash away, out of sight!

Seashells whisper silly rhymes,
To every crab who checks the times.
Laughter drifts on salty climes,
As sea foam hops and lightly climbs!

**Echoes of the Abyss**

In the depth, a dolphin chats,
About the latest swimming mats.
Squids juggle fish, oh fancy fats,
What's next? They'll wear our hats!

An octopus cooks with eight spoons,
Crafting dishes to funky tunes.
With bubbles floating like balloons,
Dinner's served under full moons!

Clownfish jest with colorful quips,
While sea urchins do silly flips.
The deep sea's filled with laughs and nips,
As everyone shares their fun trips!

Ghostly echoes, a gurgle and giggle,
Blubbery sounds and a wiggle.
Who knew the deep could make you wiggle?
With every splash, joy starts to jiggle!

## Crescendo of the Distant Shore

Pelicans pass a beachside treat,
Juggling fish while tapping feet.
With every splash, they can't be beat,
Fishermen frown, 'Oh, take a seat!'

Seashells hold a rap battle near,
Snails with bling, oh let's give a cheer!
Land crabs breakdance, so sincere,
While starfish giggle, 'We're quite clear!'

Under the sun, each cast and dive,
Creates laughter, keeps joy alive.
With each wave, the fun will thrive,
As waves dance high, we start to jive!

Back to the shore, a joyful race,
Everyone else is in our space.
The ocean's call, such a silly place,
With laughter that we all embrace!

## **Secrets in the Shells**

In a shell I found a rhyme,
It said, "Don't waste your time!"
A crab nearby just laughed so loud,
And then he danced, so proud.

With whispers from the waves, they tease,
Each tide brings out new stories, please!
A dolphin winked and flipped around,
While seagulls twisted up a sound.

The starfish wearing shades so bright,
Said, "I'm the star of every night!"
While clams just rolled their eyes in jest,
And laughed at us, their noisy guests.

So gather 'round and hear the tales,
Of laughing fish and prancing snails,
In hidden depths where secrets dwell,
Life's just a game — oh, can't you tell!

## Echoes of the Estuary

In the estuary, fish do waltz,
While shrimps claim they found some faults.
"You danced too close to my fine tail!"
Said one with a flippered flail.

The pelicans have quite a flair,
For dropping catch with quite a scare,
A fish exclaimed, with all its might,
"Why'd you spoil my dinner fight?"

Amidst the rushes, frogs will croak,
Their ribbits light as silly smoke,
They act like they run the whole show,
But who knows? They just might be slow!

The tides come in with bloops and squeaks,
While otters giggle as they peak.
With every splash, a chuckle flows,
As life here's just one big, fun show!

## **Ripples of Serenity**

The waves roll in with silly charms,
Each splash a giggle, soft alarms.
A turtle grins, "I'm on my way!"
While barnacles just block the bay.

A fish in bow tie says, "Fear not!"
"Life's just a game! Let's tie the knot!"
With bubbles giggling as they rise,
Swirling like a dance in disguise.

A solo crab starts to tap dance,
While clams can't help but steal a glance,
They blink and hide in shells, bemused,
A comedy club they've confused!

So as the sunset starts to glow,
The ripples laugh, putting on a show.
With every flick, a light-hearted tune,
As night falls soft, beneath the moon.

## The Calm Sea's Lullaby

A jellyfish floats with quite a sway,
Singing tunes for the end of the day.
The fish join in with glee and flair,
As crabs roll over without a care.

"Hey, did you hear the one about,
The shark who was a little pout?"
He thought he was the king of the sea,
But lost his crown to a bumblebee!

The tides keep rhythm, a playful beat,
As silly seaweed starts to greet.
They dance along with coral bright,
In a comical underwater light.

So hush now, listen to the sound,
Where laughter echoes all around.
For in this calm, whimsical sway,
Life's funnier than a cabaret!

## Tidepool Harmonies

In a tidepool, crabs dance, oh so spry,
With seaweed wigs, they give it a try.
A flounder swims by, calls it a show,
And a starfish claps, 'Hey, let's go slow!'

A jellyfish floats with a grin so wide,
While sea urchins sit, with spines full of pride.
The snail says, 'Wait! Is this a parade?'
But a fish splashes in, and the plans just fade.

A clam hears a joke, but it can't share,
Its shell just clanks, gasps for some air.
The sea cucumber winks with a nod,
"Life under waves? It's fairly odd!"

So next time you peek, at the pools of the shore,
Remember the laughter, and always explore.
For beneath the blue, where the giggles unfold,
The tidepool's secret is worth more than gold.

## Celestial Currents

A fish in a tux, with a top hat so neat,
Cries, "Look at me, I'm dressed for a feast!"
The current rolls by, in a swirling dance,
And a grouper shouts, "Hey, give me a chance!"

The dolphins dive deep, play peek-a-boo,
While seahorses gossip, fresh out of the blue.
"Mysteries of life," one octopus sighs,
As it twirls ink clouds, and looks to the skies.

The plankton glow bright like stars far away,
They twinkle and giggle at the end of the day.
A crab pulls the rug, in a shell-tertainment,
And all fish unite in a dance of enchantment.

So if you are drifting on ripples of light,
Join the fish party, give laughter some flight.
The waves hum the tune of their lives in the tide,
In these heavenly depths, where the sea creatures glide.

## The Whispering Waves

The waves whisper secrets, oh what a tease,
As a whale splashes by, 'I'm just here for cheese!'
The sea foam giggles, tickles the shore,
While barnacles chant, "Come back for some more!"

A lazy old turtle rolls over a stone,
Says, "Don't mind my shell, I'm just home alone."
The gulls are a chorus, loud and so brash,
While anemones sway in a colorful flash.

The tides play a song, with rhythm and cheer,
As a school of small fish whirls round in a sphere.
"Hey, watch your fins!" cries a clam with a pout,
"Not each day we get this wild whirl going out!"

So listen closely, to the waves as they laugh,
For there's humor aplenty in the ocean's half.
With every new splash, another giggle born,
Nature's jesters are out, making waves at the dawn.

## Glistening Galaxies

Beneath the surface, glimmers and glows,
Starfish in sunglasses, strike funny poses.
Fishes in sequins swim past in a line,
"Who wore it better?" they giggle, divine!

A crab with a camera clicks snaps 'round the reef,
While a clownfish grins, "I'm beyond belief!"
The coral acts shy, but blooms with bright grace,
As a turtle swims in, all speed and no pace.

The moonbeams twinkle, a celestial show,
While a whale sings softly, a bass with a flow.
"Did you hear my last hit? I'm topping the charts!"
But the crab rolls his eyes, "Try less with the farts!"

So bask in the gleam of the watery night,
Where laughter and joy make the stars all the bright.
In glistening galaxies, so wild and so free,
Life's a grand joke that's just waiting for glee.

## **Shoreside Serenade**

Seagulls squawk in crazy flight,
They steal my chips, what a sight!
Waves come crashing with a cheer,
Where's my sunscreen? It's not here!

Sandcastles fall with every tide,
The bucket spills, I can't abide.
Children laughing, dogs at play,
Beach days make me lose my way!

Umbrella flips, it takes a spin,
A sunburn? Well, that's quite the win!
Flip-flops dance across the shore,
I trip and stumble—who needs more?

Crabs that march and scuttle about,
They wave their claws, without a doubt.
As the sunset paints the sky,
I'll sing this tune until I die!

## Echoes of the Nautilus

Bubbles rise with little pops,
I wear my snorkel; who needs chops?
Fish swim past, they look so smug,
While I fumble with a hug!

Jellyfish, oh, what a sight!
Glowing softly in the night.
Trying to dance, I slip and fall,
The ocean giggles, it knows all.

Mermaids singing 'neath the waves,
Calling sailors, none are brave.
I join in with a fishy tune,
It's a concert—where's the moon?

Octopuses, what a crew!
They wave their arms, but I'm lost too.
In the deep where laughter swells,
These ocean echoes, oh, they tell!

## Swells and Skylines

Surfers wipe out, splash down hard,
I sit and watch, it's my backyard.
The sun is bright, my drink is cold,
This beach life never gets old!

Kites in the sky flutter and dash,
As I sunbathe, avoiding the splash.
Sand in my sandwich, oh what a treat,
This funny feast can't be beat!

Children shriek and run to the tide,
While I search for treasures, can't hide my pride.
Seashells glimmer like lost little dreams,
In this shoreline of giggles and gleams.

As sunset kisses the water fine,
I'll dance with shadows and sip on brine.
The swells may crash with laughter loud,
In this ocean haven, I'm so proud!

## Aquatic Anthem

Floaties bob like a merry crew,
I'll race a dolphin—me or you?
Water guns aim, the splash is grand,
I'm the ruler of this wet land!

Seaweed hair is all the rage,
I'm a fashion icon, center stage!
Starfish stand in a row so neat,
Wiggly worms, they can't be beat!

Beach balls fly and airbags pop,
I'll do a cannonball, then flop.
Sea turtles wave, all in good fun,
Join my anthem, oh, everyone!

At the end of the day, we'll toast,
With salty snacks we love the most.
A quirky tune, I'll sing with glee,
In this watery world, so wild and free!

## Currents of Memory

A crab dances funny in the sand,
Waving its claws like a tiny band.
Fish gossip in bubbles, oh what a sight,
As they plan their next oceanic fight.

Seagulls squawk jokes from up in the sky,
Trying to catch that wave passing by.
Starfish play poker, chips made of shells,
While octopuses share their tall tales.

Jellyfish jiggle, they're light on their feet,
Doing the limbo with moves so sweet.
Crabs get all tangled, but never complain,
In this underwater hilarity train.

The tide pulls a prank by shifting the sand,
Could it be planned by a fishy band?
Giggling waves crash, oh what a spree,
Creating a circus beneath a tall sea.

## Vibrations of the Shoreline

A dolphin debates with a wise old whale,
Whose stories of woe always seem to derail.
Seashells collect secrets, chattering fast,
Echoing laughter from moments long past.

Barnacles brag, they're glued to the best,
While the sunbathers tan, striving for rest.
Waves whisper jokes in a bubbly tone,
As the tide plays tricks on the old driftwood throne.

Sandcastles wobble with grace, oh so bold,
When the tide's humor turns over the gold.
Flipping their roofs, the castles declare,
"Did we just get hoisted by our own prayer?"

Seagulls perform stand-up, plucking for crumbs,
Setting the stage, they make all the puns.
With each soaring dive, laughter ignites,
At the shoreline's delight, the fun invites.

## Whirlpools of Emotion

A clam tells its tales with great starry eyes,
While the seaweed giggles in shimmering ties.
A lobster looking dapper, has quite the flair,
Cracks jokes at the party—I'm sure he'll share!

Whirlpools twirl secrets, a dance in the blue,
As fish roll with laughter, they're quite the crew.
With a flick of its tail, the shark sings a tune,
While starfish tap dance under the light of the moon.

The otters splash merrily, a comical sight,
Rolling on kelp as they bath in the light.
Their clam-flavored punchline hits hard like a wave,
We giggle and snort, can't help but misbehave.

Turtles hold court with soft gentle grins,
Laughing about how the fun never thins.
With each wave that crashes, they know it's a jest,
In the whirlpools of laughter, we're surely the best!

## **Serenade of the Seafoam**

The seafoam sings softly in playful hues,
Reciting light verses, sharing the news.
Fish play the sax while clams keep the beat,
As sea stars shimmy, it's quite the treat!

Bubbles are popping, quite like tickles inside,
Making swimmers giggle, unable to hide.
Shrimp in tuxedos are ready to dance,
As the frothy waves give the floor a chance.

Join in the fun with a splash and a dive,
With friendly sea critters, you'll feel alive.
A conch gives a shout, "Come roll with the tide!"
In this underwater carnival, joy's our guide.

The seahorses trot to their own funky beat,
While crabs take the stage, tapping their feet.
In the foam's serenade, laughter takes flight,
Together we twirl under the moon's light.

## Beneath the Briny Veil

Beneath the waves, the fish all dance,
They wear a hat and take a chance.
A crab in shades, a jellyfish prance,
They've formed a band, given half a glance.

Seagulls sing in a high-pitched tune,
While starfish twirl beneath the moon.
With glee, they hop, they giggle, they croon,
As bubbles rise like a gooey balloon.

The seaweed sways with a wave and a wink,
A dolphin dives in a playful blink.
They join the fun, not stopping to think,
Life's a splash in the salty pink.

So if you hear a bubbling cheer,
It's just the sea creatures drawing near.
Throw in a joke, bring laughter here,
In this watery world, there's nothing to fear.

## Meditations by the Marina

On a dock by the splash, all the fish wear ties,
And the octopus shows off its four fancy eyes.
Crabs are doing yoga beneath the clear skies,
While seagulls trade gossip, exchanging every prize.

A pelican with swagger steals all the snacks,
While turtles in shades chill, inside their shell tracks.
The funny fish gather and tell crazy hacks,
Each wave brings laughter; they're never out of whacks.

Frogs croak a tune that makes everyone roar,
While clams crack jokes on the slippery shore.
With each tidal laugh, there's always more in store,
In this splashy world, we forget all our chores.

So raise a glass, join the splash party's spree,
With every wave, let loose and just be.
The sea's humor flows, wild and free,
As the world drifts away like a tossed-out key.

## The Ballad of the Brine

In the brine, where the laughter flows,
A clam named Sam strikes a comical pose.
He tells tall tales and the funny fish knows,
While the sun casts a cheer that always glows.

A group of squids plays a hitchhike game,
As dolphins dive in, shouting, "Join the fame!"
They juggle shells, bringing giggles with came,
Spinning and swirling, it's all quite the same.

Octopuses arm wrestle with whirlpool might,
While krill in a chorus sing songs of delight.
All join the fun, from morning till night,
It's a splash of humor, a true sea light.

So raise your fins, take a dive down deep,
Where the laughter blooms, and the jokes never sleep.
The water sparkles, as far as we leap,
In this wacky world, where the funny waves creep.

**Algae and Anthem**

Amongst the algae, where the sea slugs slide,
The clumsy sea horses decide to collide.
With laughter and giggles, they dance on the tide,
A joyful anthem that's hard to decide.

Sharks hum along in a toothy refrain,
While fish in a line try a conga chain.
They wiggle and giggle, despite their great pain,
In the saltwater concert, there's never a feign.

The barnacles sing, with a rhythm so grand,
As snorkelers chuckle, their feet in the sand.
Each wave's a note in this oceanic band,
With laughter the secret they all understand.

So if you dive in, bring your silliest grin,
Let bubbles rise high as the jokes begin.
In a world filled with joy, there's always a win,
Join in the fun, and let the antics spin!

www.ingramcontent.com/pod-product-compliance
Lightning Source LLC
Chambersburg PA
CBHW070007300426
43661CB00141B/363